FENTON HOUSE

Hampstead

National Trust

Acknowledgements

This guidebook reflects the considerable research undertaken by Sheila Wilson into the numerous owners of Fenton House.

Tracey Avery has contributed the porcelain entries and the section on George Salting, Millicent Salting and Lady Binning. Mimi Waitzman has kindly commented on the keyboard instrument entries and the piece on Major Benton Fletcher. I have also benefited greatly from the advice and assistance of Christopher Wall, Alastair Laing, Sallyann Hardwick, Nicola Avery and Anthony du Boulay.

Anthea Palmer, 2000

In this revised edition I am grateful for the contribution of Peyton Skipwith and Michael Lee and the continuing research of Sheila Wilson.

Jane Ellis, 2008

Photographs: Birmingham Museum & Art Gallery p.25; Country Life Picture Library p.28; Getty Images/John Downing p.32; London Metropolitan Archives/Viscount Gough p.24; Mary Evans Picture Library p.5 (bottom); MWK Photography p.27; National Trust/Vera Collingwood back cover; NT/David Watson pp.8 (left and right), 9, 10 (bottom), 11 (bottom), 23; National Trust Images: Matthew Antrobus front cover, p.7, Jonathan Gibson pp.10 (top), 15, 19, John Hammond pp.4, 29 (bottom), Jerry Harpur p.22, Angelo Hornak p.1, Nadia Mackenzie pp.12, 21, 29, 31, Dick Makin p.5 (top). Derrick E. Witty pp.11 (top), 13, 14, 16, 17, 18, 30; Ian Rhind p.26.

Typeset from disc and designed by James Shurmer
Printed by Acorn Press, Swindon for National Trust (Enterprises) Ltd, Heelis, Kemble Drive, Swindon, Wilts SN2 2NA on Cocoon Silk made from 100% recycled paper

(*Front cover*) The fine gates were added in the early eighteenth century by Joshua and Anna Gee, whose initials they bear

(*Title-page*) An early Meissen grotesque teapot

(*Back cover*) The kitchen garden

Bibliography

AVERY, Tracey, 'Four Georges: The Decorative Art Collection of Mrs David Gubbay and Lady Binning', *Apollo*, April 1999, pp.16–19.

BECK, Thomasina, 'Embroidery at Fenton House', *Embroidery*, xxxvi, no.5, spring 1986, pp.12–13.

BELCHER, J., and M. Macartney, *Later Renaissance Architecture in England*, i, 1901, pp.20–2.

COUTTS, Howard, 'Champion of Fine Porcelain', *The Antique Collector*, December 1990, pp.85–90 (Lady Binning's bequest of porcelain from her mother's collection to the Royal Museum of Scotland).

DU BOULAY, Anthony, 'The Blue Porcelain Room, Fenton House: Lady Binning's Inheritance from her Uncle, George Salting', *Oriental Art*, xliv, no.2, 1998, pp.4–7.

A History of the County of Middlesex (Victoria History of the Counties of England), ix, *Hampstead and Paddington Parishes*, 1989, pp.17, 23, 27, 33.

GOTCH, J. Alfred, *The Growth of the English House: A Short History of its Architectural Development from 1100 to 1800*, 1909, pp.249–51, 255.

Hampstead Antiquarian and Historical Society Transactions, 1899, p.103.

LEE, Michael, 'Charles Ginner: Two decades portraying Flask Walk', *Flask Walk, NW3*, pp.29–42.

LEES-MILNE, James, *Caves of Ice*, 1983, p.178; *Midway on the Waves*, 1985, repr. 1996, pp.324, 333, 361; *Prophesying Peace*, 1977, pp.146, 168.

LONGFIELD, Ada K., 'Samuel Dixon's Embossed Pictures of Flowers and Birds', *Quarterly Bulletin of the Irish Georgian Society*, xviii, no.4, October–December 1974.

MAXWELL, Anna, *Hampstead*, 1912, pp.168–70.

MEW, Egan, 'The Embossed Pictures of Samuel Dixon', *Apollo*, September 1931, pp.148–53.

NARES, Gordon, 'Fenton House, Hampstead: A Home of Lady Binning', *Country Life*, 24 March 1950, pp.802–6.

SKIPWITH, Peyton, 'The Peter Barkworth Collection at Fenton House, Hampstead', *British Art Journal*, Spring 2008.

THOMPSON, F. M. L., *Hampstead: Building a Borough 1650–1964*, 1974, p.184.

WAITZMAN, Mimi S., *Early Keyboard Instruments*, pp.32–4.

WILLS, Geoffrey, 'Lady Binning's Porcelain – 1', *Connoisseur*, cxxxvii, March 1956, pp.88–91.

CONTENTS

FENTON HOUSE AND HAMPSTEAD

'A village, revelling in varieties'

A steeple issuing from a leafy rise,
With farmy fields in front, and sloping green.
Dear Hampstead, is thy southern face serene,
Silently smiling on approaching eyes.
Within, thine ever-shifting looks surprise, –
Streets, hills and dells, trees overhead now seen,
Now down below, with smoking roofs between,

A village, revelling in varieties.
Then northward what a range, – with heath and pond,
Nature's own ground; woods that let mansions through,
And cottaged vales with pillowy fields beyond,
And clump of darkening pines, and prospects blue,
And that clear path through all, where daily meet
Cool cheeks, and brilliant eyes, and morn-elastic feet.

Leigh Hunt, 'Description of Hampstead' (1815)

Since at least the seventeenth century, the village of Hampstead has drawn visitors such as Leigh Hunt up from the City of London, attracted by the expanses of the Heath, the hill air, and the water from the local wells. The wells were first publicised as early as 1653 for the medicinal properties of their iron-rich water. At the beginning of the eighteenth century, they were turned into a commercial enterprise, with a Pump Room and Great Room for assemblies. The popularity of Hampstead encouraged its expansion westward across the Heath towards Frognal, and Fenton House was built, probably about 1686, by William Eades, as part of this development.

However, the proximity to London created problems and, according to a visitor in 1724, 'brings so many loose Women in vampt-up old Clothes to catch the City Apprentices, that modest Company are ashamed to appear here'. While the wells' reputation diminished, Hampstead was established as somewhere lived in by the middle class rather than the fashionable. As Daniel Defoe wrote in 1724:

Hampstead indeed is risen from a little Country Village, to a City, not upon the Credit only of the Waters, tho' this apparent; its growing Greatness began there, but Company increasing gradually, and the People liking both the Place and the Diversions together, it grew suddenly Populous, and the Concourse of People was Incredible.

Fenton House's early owners were typical of the middle-class professional inhabitants of Hampstead: Thomas Simpson lawyer, Joshua Gee linen merchant, John Hyndman tobacco importer, James Fenton Baltic merchant (who gave his name to the house), Thomas Turner lawyer, and George Trewby gas engineer.

In 1774 the Heath was described as adorned with many gentleman's houses. Individual large houses were still being built until the middle of the nineteenth century, when more modest houses became popular. Fenton House remained remarkably untouched either by these developments or its numerous owners. It is still, as it was in 1756, 'a substantial brick building ... a pleasant garden well

*James Fenton,
an early owner*

Fenton House from Hampstead Grove; a nineteenth-century engraving of how it might have looked in the 1780s

planted with Fruit-Trees, and a Kitchen-Garden all inclos'd with a substantial Brick Wall'.

From the early eighteenth century, Hampstead had been popular with writers such as Keats and Leigh Hunt and artists such as Constable. It is perhaps fitting then that after so many professional owners, Fenton House should come into the hands of the art-loving Katherine, Lady Binning and be filled with her fine collections of porcelain, pictures, needlework and furniture. Lady Binning left the house in 1952 to the National Trust, which in turn placed here the Benton Fletcher Collection of early keyboard instruments, and, more recently, the Peter Barkworth (1929–2006) collection of British pictures and paintings.

In Visscher's 1616 View of London, *Hampstead appears as a wooded hill with two windmills. Fenton was built about 70 years later near the left-hand mill*

TOUR OF THE HOUSE

The Exterior

THE SOUTH FRONT

Most visitors approach the house from the south up Holly Hill. This way in is marked by a wrought-iron gate which bears the initials of Joshua Gee and his wife Anna, who lived here from 1706 to 1730. It is of unusually high quality and appears to have been made by a craftsman working under the direct influence of the great ironworker Jean Tijou, who was in England from 1689 to 1712 and designed gates for Hampton Court and St Paul's Cathedral. In 1899 there were still local people who remembered these gates being used by sedan chairs going to and from the parish church.

The south front displays many of the building's characteristics. The material used is a deep brownish brick, with rubbed red brick for the dressings, including the window frames and corner quoins. A plain projecting band, or string course, runs between the two principal floors. Under the widely projecting eaves is a boldly carved wooden cornice typical of several in Hampstead that date from the early eighteenth century, of which Burgh House in Well Walk is a good example. It is the roof that perhaps most clearly suggests that the house was designed by a master carpenter or brick-layer such as the father of William Eades, who may have built the house, rather than by one of the very small circle of professional architects active in London in the 1680s. Instead of a rectangular platform with a cupola on top of the roof, of the type recommended by the architectural writer Sir Roger Pratt, there are instead two small balustraded flat roofs, or platforms, over the projecting wings on the east front, from each of which rises a full chimneystack. The south front clearly shows the resulting asymmetrical pitch of the main roof.

The arrangement of the south front reflects the disposition and uses of the interior. The three centre bays project very slightly and are surmounted by a pediment; the doorcase is also pedimented, on Doric pilasters. This door leads into the Dining Room, previously a garden hall, on the ground floor. At each end of the first floor there are slender windows to what were small closets off the main rooms. The dormer windows light two of the attic rooms, while the basement windows indicate the extent of that floor.

THE EAST FRONT

The colonnaded porch was added, probably by James Fenton after 1807, in the space between the two chimneystacks. Access was clearly more immediate from Hampstead Grove than from Holly Hill, and this was always the principal entrance to the house. Above it can be seen the circular dial where there was a clock: it was called Clock House from about 1760 until some time in the nineteenth century. The windows at each end of the ground and first floors all light closets.

THE NORTH FRONT

The north front is dominated by the tall central window that lights the staircase and rather awkwardly cuts through the string course. Its thick glazing bars are amongst the few remaining from the 1680s; most of the others were replaced with a thinner pattern in the eighteenth century. It is also on this side that the drop in ground level makes the basement windows fully visible. Viewed from the Terrace Walk, the full scale of the house can be appreciated.

The south front

THE WEST FRONT

By 1901 the west front had been extended to add a cloakroom and a bathroom on the ground and first floors respectively. While there is no public access to the service yard on the western side of the house, this addition can be seen from the Kitchen Garden. Also visible is the Coach House, which accommodated two coaches and eight horses in 1756. In 1920 it housed two cars and only three horses, perhaps suggesting that the building had by then been reduced in size. Servants lived above.

The Interior

Excluding the extension on the west front, the ground plan is a perfect square, originally split into quarters by a central cross, of which two arms contain the principal and secondary staircases, and another the present Hall. Each of the four rooms on the two principal floors had closets, many with tiny windowless cupboards leading off them, where close-stools (lavatories) would have been kept. Unusually, several rooms that can never have been bedrooms, such as the Dining Room, had closets.

For more specific information on the porcelain collection than is given in the following tour, please ask to see the room information sheets. There is a separate book of the musical instruments.

THE HALL

The hall runs from the front to the back of the house, with a door across to shut off the service staircase. It has some original seventeenth-century panelling, while the frieze is of about 1810.

PICTURES

The two pictures by Charles Ginner (1878–1952), *Flask Walk, Hampstead Night* (*c.*1920) and *Pond Street*, are from Peter Barkworth's bequest (see p.32). Charles Ginner was brought up in the south of France and trained first as an architect and then as a painter at the Academie Vitti in Paris. In 1910 his work was shown at the Allied Artists' Association in the Albert Hall. Because the hanging was alphabetical, he was brought together with Harold Gilman and Spencer Gore, artists with whom he founded the Camden Town Group. He favoured urban scenes, paying immense attention to the textures of bricks and tiles and, after his move to Hampstead in 1919, drew and painted the view from his studio window down Flask Walk at least nineteen times.

The oval portrait is of James Fenton (1754–1834), who lived in the house from 1806 until 1834 and after whom it is probably named.

FURNITURE

This includes two walnut late seventeenth-century chairs with cane backs and seats and a long-case clock made about 1700 by James Shiel of Earlestown (Lancashire) in a contemporary walnut case with cross-banding.

THE DINING ROOM

This was originally two rooms. The part of the room with the harpsichord was a morning room, with a closet in what is now an alcove. The other end was, as now, a dining room, which still has its original closet. Between 1920 and 1936 the communicating double doors between what are now the Drawing Room and Blue Porcelain Room were moved downstairs and inserted in the walls between the Morning Room and Dining Room. The National Trust enlarged this opening to create the present arrangement. The decoration and curtains date from John Fowler's refurbishment of the house in 1973–4.

CERAMICS

On the chimneypiece at the western (right-hand) end are two Chinese *famille verte* coloured vases of

the Kangxi period (1662–1722). At the other end of the room are two English early nineteenth-century earthenware cockerels. The wall-mounted Chinese dishes decorated in *famille rose* colours date from the Qianlong period (1736–95). The earthenware pieces on the sideboard are early nineteenth-century English.

PICTURES

Several of the paintings in this room are by William Nicholson and are on loan from the family of the late T. W. Bacon (1873–1950), who formed the collection. He made his first acquisition in 1905 and his last in 1930, when the collection amounted to over 30 oil paintings as well as various watercolours and engravings.

FURNITURE

The needlework pole-screen and eight carved mahogany dining-chairs date from the eighteenth century. Two of a set of lyre-back chairs, a pair of console tables supported on a single foot, and a wine-cooler made of yew in the shape of a classical sarcophagus, under the sideboard, are all Regency.

MUSICAL INSTRUMENTS

A Shudi and Broadwood harpsichord of 1770. Established in Soho, Burkat Shudi took on John Broadwood as an apprentice in 1761. Their collaboration grew into the famous Broadwood firm. This harpsichord is the earliest surviving with both partners' names on the nameboard. It was the largest and most elaborate model of harpsichord ever made in England. It was also the one that seems to have most influenced music in continental European courts. Of the dozen examples that survive, the most famous was despatched to the Prussian court after having been played by the young Mozart on his visit to London in 1765. This harpsichord is said to have been made for one Dr Hartley, a friend of Samuel Taylor Coleridge.

In the alcove on the left is a *1774 Broadwood square piano* left by David Wainwright to the National Trust. Enormously popular throughout the late eighteenth century and much of the nineteenth, these rectangular instruments served the function in the home of today's upright pianos.

(Far left)
Flask Walk;
by Charles Ginner
(Hall)

(Left)
Francis and
Christopher
Bacon; *by William*
Nicholson (Dining
Room)

(Right)
The Shudi and
Broadwood
harpsichord in the
Dining Room

THE PORCELAIN ROOM

This room was variously described in the late nineteenth century and early twentieth century as the Small Smoking Room, Study and Sitting Room. For a brief moment before 1936 it became the Kitchen with a scullery to the right of the fireplace and a pantry to the left. When Dr Abercrombie rented the house from Lady Binning in 1937–9, he used it as his surgery.

The cabinets were designed by Geddes Heslop for the National Trust in order to accommodate porcelain which Lady Binning had had out on open display or in display cabinets which left the house. The decoration and curtains all date from John Fowler's refurbishment of the house in 1973–4.

CERAMICS

The two alcove cases either side of the chimney-breast display some of the finest figures produced by a range of English and continental factories of the eighteenth century, which allow for comparison of styles and influences. The right-hand cabinet features a number of early Meissen figures sculpted in the lively Baroque style of the 1740s by Meissen's greatest master-modeller Johann Joachim Kändler (1706–75). Note his cheeky harlequins, which were conceived to be viewed from all sides, originally as part of elaborate table decorations at the Dresden court of Augustus the Strong. The Meissen pieces are ably supported by key examples of similar subjects from the other major German factories.

The Meissen figure of Harlequin was designed as a table decoration, to be viewed from all sides

Notable figures and groups include Scaramouche, modelled by Franz Anton Bustelli (1723–64) for Nymphenburg, and Mezzetin and Isabella, modelled by Johann Christoph Ludwig von Lücke for Höchst, c.1752.

The diversity of Lady Binning's collection is evident in the left-hand cabinet, which displays both hard- and soft-paste pieces from the earliest English porcelain factories. A remarkable series of Bristol figures (for example, the set of Rustic Seasons, c.1773–4), exhibits a greyish tone characteristic of English hard-paste.

Among the better-known factories producing

*(Left)
A Bristol set of the Rustic Seasons, c.1773–4*

*(Right)
La ci Darem la Mano; by Walter Sickert, 1937*

soft-paste porcelain in England, Bow, Chelsea and Derby are represented in the left-hand cabinet. Some figures of the Chelsea gold anchor period (1758–77), such as the Imperial Shepherd and Shepherdess (c.1765), were probably modelled by Joseph Willems, loosely based on Meissen originals and framed with a distinctive 'bocage' of flowers. Figures from this showy period of Chelsea's manufacture are a feature of numerous collections formed in the early twentieth century. Rarer is the Longton Hall figure of Harlequin, c.1755 (also after a Meissen model), purchased by Lady Binning in 1939. Between the windows is an inkstand composed of Meissen porcelain figures, probably from the 1760s, mounted in French ormolu.

PICTURES

Above the harpsichord hangs a *La ci Darem la Mano* (1937) by Walter Sickert (1860–1942), part of Peter Barkworth's collection.

The set of seven bird and two flower pictures was produced by Samuel Dixon (d. 1769), using a method he claimed as his own, which involved

An embossed flower picture by Samuel Dixon

embossing paper to create a relief effect and then colouring it in gouache. Dixon had a shop in Capel Street, Dublin, from where he advertised these pictures (a full set of which numbered twelve) as 'useful to paint and draw after, or imitate in Shell or Needle Work'. The flower pictures were published in 1748 and proved so popular that they were followed in 1750 by a bird set. These were derived from the first four volumes of George Edwards's *Natural History of Uncommon Birds* (1743–51).

FURNITURE

Between the windows hangs a fine gilt gesso mirror, or sconce, once equipped with branches for candles, made about 1715 in the style of Gumley and Moore. The mirror above the mantelpiece is mid-Georgian. The armchair of the Sheraton period has exceptionally fine painted decoration of flowers and cornucopiae (horns of plenty).

MUSICAL INSTRUMENT

A Johannes Ruckers harpsichord of 1612, on loan from Her Majesty the Queen, and formerly at Windsor Castle. This double-manual instrument by a member of a famous Antwerp family of harpsichord-makers was enlarged in England in the eighteenth century. Fortunately, the original soundboard with its authentic Ruckers rose and fruit and floral decoration survives intact.

*(Right)
Valentine Snow
was the leading
trumpeter of the
mid-eighteenth
century; his
portrait hangs on
the Staircase*

THE ORIENTAL ROOM

Lady Binning used this room as a library, and a photograph taken in her time shows it furnished with comfortable armchairs, but otherwise much as it is today. Again, the alcove originally contained a separate closet, but this division had gone by 1936, when it was also a library. While the paintwork is a John Fowler scheme, the curtains and window cushions are later renewals.

CERAMICS

The Oriental Room houses a range of early Chinese ceramics mainly bought by Lady Binning in the late 1920s and early 1930s. Along the upper shelves of the English Chinese Chippendale-style cabinet are pieces from the Song dynasty (960–1279), delicately carved or moulded under a bluish-white Qingbai glaze and the whiter glaze of Dingyao ware. Stronger coloured glazes of the Ming dynasty (1368–1644) can be seen in the Imperial yellow saucer dish and the saucer depicting two phoenixes in green enamel on a *rouge-de-fer* or coral-coloured ground, both from the Jiajing period (1522–66), and the *wucai* (five colours) vase decorated with boys playing ('wa wa' subjects) from the period of Wanli (1573–1619).

On the mantelpiece are several Dehua joss-stick holders in the form of Dogs of Fo of the Kangxi period (1662–1722), decorated with a translucent white glaze known as *blanc-de-Chine*. This type of ware was imported into Europe from China in the late seventeenth and early eighteenth centuries.

FURNITURE

The two paintings on glass and the red lacquer circular tray are examples of the eighteenth-century Chinese export trade. The English red lacquer pier-glass of about 1700 still has its original plate.

SNUFF BOTTLES

These are Chinese, mostly of the Qing dynasty (1644–1911) and in porcelain, glass and hard stones.

THE STAIRCASE

The Staircase still has its original seventeenth-century twisted balusters, and is lit by an unusually large, but also apparently unchanged, window of ten panes by four, which overlooks the walled garden.

In Lady Binning's time, a large Flemish tapestry of the story of David and Abigail hung here. To furnish the large bare walls, John Fowler hung the 'Prickly Pear' pattern wallpaper you see today. New carpet was laid in 1974, copying a design at Hardwick Hall in Derbyshire.

PICTURES

On the Staircase hang portraits which were given to the National Trust by Major Clarence Goff with his home, The Courts, Holt, in Wiltshire, from where they are on loan. Major Goff's son Tom was an important collector and maker of early keyboard instruments – a fitting link with Fenton House and the Benton Fletcher Collection. As you climb the stairs, there are portraits of Lord Frederick and Lord Adolphus Fitzclarence, the natural sons of William IV from his liaison with the actress Mrs Jordan before he became king. Major Goff was a grandson of their brother, Lord Augustus. The Hart Davis family, who lived here during the nineteenth century, were descended from William and Mrs Jordan through a daughter. The trumpeter is thought to represent Valentine Snow and, if true, would have been painted around 1753. Snow was the most famous player of his day, performing at the first nights of many of Handel's operas. He was Sergeant Trumpeter to the Royal Household from 1753 and died in 1770. The portrait of George IV, older brother of William IV, is by Thomas Beach (1738–1806). The portrait of William IV when Duke of Clarence is a version of the original by Sir Thomas Lawrence (1769–1830).

The picture of a horse and jockey is in the manner of George Stubbs (1724–1806).

CERAMICS

The glazed cabinet at the top of the landing on the main stairs contains a selection of early nineteenth-century English pottery animal figures and Toby jugs, which were probably collected by Lady Binning or her mother, Millicent Salting.

THE ROCKINGHAM ROOM

This has always been a bedroom, and still has its original closet. There was also once a jib-door into what is now the Blue Porcelain Room. It was called the Blue Room in Lady Binning's day; its present name reflects the Rockingham china now here.

CERAMICS

The eighteenth-century models of animals (here from Rockingham, Chelsea and Bow) can be compared with the less sophisticated nineteenth-century English pottery in the cabinet on the landing. The identifiable pieces from the Rockingham factory include a pair of figures of a ram and a sheep on shaped oval bases with coloured flowers in relief.

PICTURES

Over the mantelpiece hangs a view of Hampstead Heath after John Constable (1776–1837), which was once part of George Salting's collection. To the right of the fireplace is a print of *The Sea Monster* or *The Rape of Amymone* by Albrecht Dürer (1471–1528). The original engraving was executed just before 1500, but this impression dates from about 1525. To the left of the closet door are two pictures by John Constable (1776–1837), *Cumulus Clouds over a Landscape* (*c*.1822) and *Seascape with Shipping*, and two by his contemporary David Cox (1783–1859), *Beaumaris* and *Cottage by a Pool*.

NEEDLEWORK PICTURES

In this and the Green Room can be found a wonderful collection of mainly seventeenth-century embroidered pictures. Many of them were in Mrs Salting's house at 49 Berkeley Square in 1914, but it is not clear whether she collected them herself. There was a well-documented collection of embroidery at Mellerstain, one of the Scottish homes of Lady Binning's husband. Lady Binning herself was an accomplished needlewoman.

WALL FACING FIREPLACE, LEFT TO RIGHT:

Jacob's Dream
Jacob dreams of a ladder reaching to heaven. Embroidered on ivory-coloured silk, it is very similar to a design by Marten de Vos, engraved by Gerard de Jode for an illustrated Old Testament, published in Antwerp in 1585, which circulated widely and was much copied.

King Solomon and the Queen of Sheba; seventeenth-century stump-work

King Solomon and the Queen of Sheba
Solomon looks like Charles I, and royalist symbols such as the lion can be seen. So it may be a tribute, the butterfly symbolising the rebirth of the monarchy under Charles II. It also includes a squirrel and peacocks, both of which were kept as pets at that time. Seventeenth-century stump-work or raised work.

Woman with a Flower and Man in a Garden
A canvas-work version of one of the most common scenes in seventeenth-century embroidery. It may show William of Orange and Queen Mary, who popularised the tulip in Britain – hence perhaps what seems to be a large tulip on the right.

Fitzgerald and Boyle Family 'raised work' picture
The subject is puzzling. It may show the story of Joseph and Potiphar's wife, in which she attempts unsuccessfully to seduce him. The coats of arms are those of George Fitzgerald, 16th Earl of Kildare (1611–60) and his wife Joan Boyle, daughter of the 1st Earl of Cork.

Rebecca at the Well
Rebecca is chosen as the wife for Isaac. Jacob was their son. The scene was also a popular print. Canvas-work with knot-stitch for the sheep.

Elijah and the Widow of Zanephath
A pair with *Jacob's Dream*, in the same silk-work. Elijah the Hebrew prophet, suffering from the drought he had ordained, met a widow who gave him food and drink. When her son was dying, Elijah called on God and saved his life. This scene is very like a Bible cover in the Metropolitan Museum, New York, which is based on a print by Gerard de Jode.

WALL FACING WINDOWS, LEFT TO RIGHT:

Shepherd and Shepherdess
Coarsely worked on canvas in the late seventeenth or early eighteenth century. Pastoral scenes came into vogue at this time.

Judith with the Head of Holofernes
The figures in the corners are the four Cardinal Virtues – Justice, Temperance, Fortitude and Prudence. Inscribed on the back as the work of Catherine Owen and dated 1637. An unfinished piece of silk-work, this shows how the embroiderer used a print for her design.

Woman with a Flower and Man in a Garden; late seventeenth-century canvas-work

IN CENTRE OF ROOM:

Casket
These boxes were fashionable from about 1650 to 1700 and were usually the work of young girls. Inside this one are compartments with two scent bottles, an ink vase and pounce (fine powder used to prevent ink from spreading) pot. There would have been a mirror in the top. The scene on the top is the Judgement of Paris. Round the long sides are the Four Elements, and round the short sides the story of David and Abigail, in which she brings peace offerings to him during his exile.

FURNITURE

Between the windows is a walnut bureau of about 1715, with a circular Regency mirror surmounted by an eagle above it. The two Dutch marquetry chairs have seats covered in *gros point* (cross-stitch) embroidery by Lady Binning.

MUSICAL INSTRUMENTS

A Shudi single manual harpsichord of 1761. It belonged to the pianist Fanny Davies (1861–1934), who was a pupil of Clara Schumann. She often included early keyboard music in her programmes.

In the Closet is *the Marcus Siculus virginals* of 1540. This is the oldest signed and dated instrument in the collection, and is a unique extant example of this maker's work. The decoration is confined to the surfaces which would have been shown when the instrument was sitting inside a protective wooden case (now lost).

THE BLUE PORCELAIN ROOM
(LADY BINNING'S BEDROOM)

When Lady Binning bought Fenton House, she used this room as her bedroom. As with the ground-floor rooms, there would have originally been a closet for powdering one's wig in beside the fireplace, and indeed this seems to have still been in existence in 1920. The columns were probably inserted about 1810, possibly replacing a passage wall. This passage would have led from the staircase to the mechanism of the clock, which was originally placed in the centre of the east front, and whose dial plate still exists. The northern wall, lined with shelves converted by Lady Binning to display porcelain, originally had a central jib door to the Rockingham Room.

Lady Binning's bequest to the National Trust did not include bedroom furniture, and from 1952 to 2004 this room was furnished as a music room. Using a photograph from *Country Life* magazine, the room has now been refurnished and decorated as it appeared in 1950. A generous gift has enabled the reproduction of the upholstered bed and counterpane, and the present owner of the tapestry agreed to a photographic reproduction being made.

CERAMICS

The blue-and-white porcelain of the Kangxi period (1662–1722) shows the Chinese skill at producing a rich cobalt-blue enamel colour under a brilliant translucent glaze. These fashionable products were supplied to wealthy European courts by the Dutch East India Company from the mid-seventeenth century and so increased Europeans' desire to produce their own porcelain. The Delft factories in Holland developed a successful market for reproducing blue-and-white oriental china in tin-glazed earthenware.

FURNITURE

This includes a particularly elegant small mahogany work-table with a serpentine front, incorporating a fire-screen at the back, in the Rococo style of John Cobb, and a Dutch Neo-classical marquetry commode.

MUSICAL INSTRUMENTS

The spinet was made in London, perhaps by the Hitchcock family, during the first half of the eighteenth century. The decorative ivory strip on the ebony keys is associated with this firm.

The early seventeenth-century Italian virginals was made by Vincentius of Prato near Florence in Italy. Like the Siculus virginals in the Rockingham Room Closet, it is lightly built, but its size, shape and point where the action plucks the strings give it an entirely different sound.

PICTURES

The flower picture is by N. F. Knip (1742–1809).

A portrait of George Salting shows him with a vase from his collection.

Between the window hangs *A Donor with St Christopher* by Adriaen Isenbrandt (active 1510–51), which appears to be the right wing of a diptych (two-part picture). It came from George Salting's collection (see p.30).

A Donor with St Christopher; *by Adriaen Isenbrandt*

THE DRAWING ROOM

This seems always to have been a drawing room. The panelling, the dentil frieze and the two arched alcoves were probably introduced early in the nineteenth century by James Fenton (or possibly his uncle, Philip). Called the China Room in Lady Binning's day, it had two pairs of full-length display cabinets.

The Judicious Lover; eighteenth-century glass-painting after Hubert Gravelot (Drawing Room)

The redecoration of this room was undertaken by John Fowler. Most striking is the flounce on the Caroline chintz curtains. This was inspired by one seen by John Fowler on the early nineteenth-century Blue Bedroom hangings at Kasteel Duivenvoorde in Holland.

CERAMICS

Whereas the Porcelain Room dramatically highlights the sculptural qualities of individual figures, the china in the Drawing Room is arranged to show how it could be used to furnish a room. On either side of the chimneybreast, the alcove shelves contain fine wares from the Worcester factory, which date from around 1770 and reveal great virtuosity in painted decoration. The splendid hexagonal vase and cover, with figures on a pink and gold scale-pattern ground, was probably decorated by a painter at an independent workshop in London. Jefferys Hammett O'Neale, a leading London decorator, painted the pair of tea bowls which depict scenes from Aesop's fables – a goat and a cow, a dog and a fox – and the large dish with a scale-blue ground.

Lady Binning commissioned the pair of satinwood cabinets, specifically to display her china. In the left-hand cabinet is the curious grotesque teapot which resembles a bearded Chinaman on a shell, modelled by Meissen's master modeller, J. J. Irminger, after Jacques Stella's *Livre des vases* (1667). As with numerous wares from Meissen, the

piece left the factory white and was later decorated by *hausmalerei* (outside decorators); in this case the gilt chinoiseries were painted in the Augsburg workshop of Abraham Seuter. Chinoiserie decoration gave way to European scenes painted in reserves, as Meissen experimented with new styles and coloured grounds. Noteworthy here is the gold-ground tea and coffee service painted with Watteau-style figure groups, c.1745.

Figures from a range of German factories, seen in the right-hand cabinet further illustrate the breadth of Mrs Salting's collection. The important pair of Frankenthal court dancers, modelled by J. F. Lück, c.1761–4, was one of the few pieces to be illustrated in her 1914 inventory. The charming pastoral groups of children are characteristic products of modellers such as Russinger and Melchior at Höchst. Mrs Salting's love of miniature and toy figures is evident from the Chelsea and Meissen examples in the satinwood secretaire.

PICTURES

To the right of the fireplace hangs an ink and coloured wash *River Landscape with Bridge and Cottages* by Jan Brueghel the Elder (1568–1625), and to the left hang two watercolours by William Marlow (1740–1813), which probably depict the Thames.

Of the five eighteenth-century pictures painted on glass, two are portraits (of Viscountess Andover and her sister, Lady Mostyn) and the others genre scenes.

Between the windows hangs the earliest textile piece in the collection, a purple velvet Elizabethan sweet bag, embroidered in silver, gold and pearls.

FURNITURE

The furniture is predominantly satinwood in the Sheraton style and includes a small secretaire-cabinet on the left-hand wall, flanked by a pair of side-tables painted with floral garlands, on one of which is placed an elaborate painted satinwood tea-caddy. A pair of chairs and two other single chairs are likewise painted satinwood of about 1800, and there are also two chests-of-drawers.

The copy of a sixteenth-century silver *nef* (a ship table ornament) is in a tortoiseshell case, possibly adapted from a clock-case.

THE GREEN ROOM

In 1920 this was a bedroom and still contained a 'Powder Closet having window and inner cupboard, fitted shelves'. In 1936 it was being used as a dressing room.

The present scheme, including the curtains, but not the carpet, was devised by the interior designer David Mlinaric.

CERAMICS

The Green Room contains a miscellany of porcelain and pottery. Of particular interest in the Dutch cabinet are the so-called *Dismal Hounds* of *c.*1758 from Bow, and two small Tournai figures. Staffordshire figures and wares are grouped on the mantelpiece. The chest-on-stand is surmounted by Chinese vases from the Kangxi period (1662–1722).

PICTURES

Above the mantelpiece hangs a portrait of James II when Duke of York, possibly by Simon Luttichuys (1610–*c.*1662/3). In the closet bay are two pictures by Francis Sartorius (1734–1804) – *Psyche* (a Persian cat, of 1787) and *A Terrier*.

NEEDLEWORK PICTURES

OUTSIDE GREEN ROOM:

The Adoration of the Magi
A panel from the Sheldon tapestry workshop, *c.*1600, in wool and silk, and gold and silver thread, so in this case woven, not sewn. William Sheldon of Barcheston, Warwickshire founded the first commercial tapestry workshop in England about 1561.

Swan Inn
Sewn in fine canvas-work. The Swan was a popular name for inns. Swans were valued for their meat and feathers as well as for their beauty – to own a bird, you had to have a licence from the Crown.

INSIDE GREEN ROOM, BETWEEN WINDOWS:

Esther and Ahasuerus
The central scene shows the Jewish Queen Esther pleading for her people before her husband, King Ahasuerus of Persia. Embroidered in various stitches, this was the most popular Old Testament theme for seventeenth-century embroiderers.

Lady and Black Page
Late seventeenth-century in *petit point* (tent-stitch).

Psyche, a Persian cat; by Francis Sartorius, 1787 (Green Room)

Portrait of a Lady with Scenes from Ovid

The motif of a black page attendant on his mistress was popular in paintings of the period.

TO RIGHT OF WINDOWS, ON EAST WALL,
LEFT TO RIGHT:

Hagar and Ishmael
Sarah, shown in her tent on the right, demanded that Abraham banish his mistress Hagar and her son Ishmael. This version of another much-embroidered Old Testament story is worked in unusually minute stitches. It is thought to be based on engravings by Gerard de Jode of 1585.

Elijah fed by Ravens and the Widow of Zarephath
Elijah in the wilderness is fed by the ravens, and later by the widow and her son.

Portrait of a Lady with Scenes from Ovid
The lady appears in many embroidered pictures. Around her are three scenes from Ovid's *Metamorphoses*: *Daphne and Apollo* (top left), *Venus and Adonis* (top right) and *Narcissus* (right side). Raised work (or stumpwork) on white satin designed to cover a casket.

Shepherd and Shepherdess
Embroidered in a variety of canvas-stitches, it is edged with silver braid. These peaceful scenes were popular after the ravages of the Civil War.

ENAMELS

These were made in Bilston, Birmingham and Staffordshire, mostly in the mid-eighteenth cen-

tury. Among them can be spotted the likenesses of George II, Sir Robert Walpole, the Duke of Cumberland and Oliver Cromwell. They were given to the Trust by Dr J. W. P. Bourke.

FURNITURE

The walnut chest-on-stand is of about 1700. The small settee, or loveseat, was probably made about 1720.

THE SERVICE STAIRCASE

The secondary stairs, like the Main Staircase, survive in their original seventeenth-century form, though with sturdy plain balusters instead of the other's more ornate balustrade, and linking all four storeys rather than just the two principal floors.

PICTURES

Twenty-eight eighteenth- and nineteenth-century drawings, watercolours and small oils from the Peter Barkworth collection include *Stoke Castle, Shropshire* by Paul Sandby (1725–1809), *San Remo, October 1865* by William Wyld (1806–1889), *Worthing Beach, 1895* by James Orrock (1829–1913) and *Sandhills Common, Witley, Surrey* by Helen Allingham (1845–1926).

At the top of the stairs hangs *Neptune's Horses*, painted by G. F. Watts (1817–1904) in 1888–92. It was inspired by watching the sea at Sliema in Malta: 'Neptune's horses seemed to be racing towards us.'

The small collection of pictures of William IV's mistress, the actress Dora Jordan, includes the pastel *Mrs Jordan Playing a Lute* by John Russell and *Mrs Jordan and another Actor in Coffey and Mottley's farce 'The Devil to Pay'*, said to be by a fellow actor, Richard Colbourn.

FURNITURE

On the landing stands a French or Italian late sixteenth-century *buffet à deux corps* (roughly the equivalent of an Elizabethan food cupboard) with a panel carved with the River God Tiber and the infants Romulus and Remus. On it are placed an Indian stringed instrument, a sarimdah, and two seventeenth-century pottery jars, a water pot and a Rhenish bellamine wine-jar with a mask of a bearded man.

THE ATTIC

The small bedrooms in the Attic were probably used originally by the family, with their servants sleeping in the basement and in buildings outside the house. By the nineteenth century these could have been used by either. Sheer numbers must have partly dictated this. Joshua Gee had nine children; Philip Fenton lived here with his nephew, wife and seven children; Richard Hart-Davis had seven adults in the house, and George Trewby had seven children. In Lady Binning's day, the housekeeper, butler and cook all had bedrooms with fireplaces on this floor; the maids' rooms had no heating.

The rooms are now used to show oil paintings from the Peter Barkworth collection and a large part of the Benton Fletcher collection of instruments.

THE NORTH-WEST ROOM

MUSICAL INSTRUMENTS

The double-manual harpsichord of 1777 made by Shudi's principal rivals, Jacob and Abraham Kirckman, exemplifies all of the typical English features, including a nag's head swell which allowed players to create the crescendo and diminuendo that were required to perform the new music being written with the piano in mind.

The spinet in the corner has an unreliable inscription of John Hancock. It was rescued by Major Fletcher from an outhouse in Wales, where he found rain falling on it, the lid 'split into a hundred pieces, and the wood warped'.

The double-manual harpsichord of 1762 by the founder of the Kirckman firm, Jacob, offers similar musical resources to the instrument of 1777 by him and his nephew, Abraham, also in this room.

PICTURES

Above the 1777 harpsichord hangs a painting by Peter Kuhfeld of a girl playing the instrument while it stood in the Blue Porcelain Room (now Lady Binning's Bedroom).

THE NORTH ROOM

MUSICAL INSTRUMENTS

On the right is *the Hatley virginal*. This is the earliest English instrument in the collection, dating from 1664. In the seventeenth century in England, 'virginals' signified plucked keyboard instruments of every shape.

Mrs Janet Leeper presented *the 1925 Arnold Dolmetsch clavichord* to the National Trust in memory of her aunt, Miss Dorothy Swainson, to whom the instrument belonged. The French motto inside the lid means 'More is achieved through gentleness than violence'. Dolmetsch was a key figure in the revival of early music in England in the early twentieth century.

THE NORTH-EAST ROOM

CERAMICS

The deer figures on the mantelpiece are English, nineteenth-century.

PICTURES

Several paintings by members of the Camden Town Group, including two Polish views by Robert Bevan, a river scene by Walter Sickert and a still-life by Harold Gilman.

Above the Broadwood piano hangs a portrait of *A Woman Sewing, 1916* by Duncan Grant.

MUSICAL INSTRUMENTS

The piano to the right bears the plausible, but fraudulent, inscription of Americus Backers, a Dutchman who settled in London and had premises in Jermyn Street in 1763–78. Though few genuine Backers instruments survive, they were highly respected by contemporaries and often faked. *The second piano* dates from 1805 and is by the famous and prolific Broadwood firm. English pianos of this period were known for the beauty and fullness of their tone, and this instrument, though smaller in compass, resembles in other respects the one given by Broadwood a decade or so later to Beethoven.

Single-strung Italian harpsichord, sixteenth or seventeenth century

THE EAST ROOM

This room is now devoted to the characters in the *Odd and Elsewhere* children's books created by James Roose-Evans, which are set at Fenton House. On the walls can be seen some of the original illustrations by Brian Robb.

THE SOUTH-EAST ROOM

PICTURES

These include *Self-portrait* by Clare Atwood (1866–1962), a painter and friend of the actress Ellen Terry, and *Rye, Sussex, 1913* by James Bolivar Manson, painted while on a working holiday with Lucien Pissarro.

MUSICAL INSTRUMENTS

To the left stands *a single-strung Italian harpsichord* in a richly painted outer case dating from the late sixteenth or early seventeenth century.

The single-manual harpsichord is by Jacob Kirckman. Dated 1752, it is the earliest of the three examples of this maker's work at Fenton House. It is rare in having just two sets of strings.

On the central table is *an eighteenth-century hurdy-gurdy*, while on the other one is *a small nineteenth century archlute*.

THE SOUTH-WEST ROOM

CERAMICS

The cow-creamers on the mantelpiece are English pottery of the late eighteenth and early nineteenth centuries.

PICTURES

A number of theatrical pictures from the Peter Barkworth collection, including *Rehearsal, Drury Lane* by Clare Atwood and *Britannia Ballet, The Alhambra, 1910* by Spencer Gore (1878–1914).

Above the clavichord are three pencil and watercolour sketches of Charles Anthony Calvert, his wife and son, by Thomas Charles Wageman (*c.*1787–1863), all of which were given to the National Trust in 1978.

MUSICAL INSTRUMENTS

The single-manual harpsichord was made in London by Thomas Culliford in 1783 and sold by Longman & Broderip, the firm founded at 26 Cheapside in the 1760s as a music publisher and dealer in musical instruments. It employed recognised makers to build instruments to its specifications.

The clavichord is thought to be German from the second half of the seventeenth century. Unlike harpsichords, spinets and virginals, which have plucked strings, those of the clavichord are struck by tangents – brass blades mounted on the backs of the keys.

The painted virginal is now believed to have been made by the famous late sixteenth- and seventeenth-century Venetian builder, Giovanni Celestini. Very unusually, it has two unison strings for each note.

THE GARDEN

HISTORY

In 1756 the garden was described as 'pleasant … well planted with Fruit-Trees, and a Kitchen-Garden, all inclos'd with a substantial Brick Wall'. By 1762 a greenhouse had been added by Mary Martin. A plan attached to an 1860 Enfranchisement confirms that the basic layout has changed little since then. To the south, a path runs up to the house through a 'lawn and flower garden'. The terrace walks to the north are there, and the garden on that side is divided into two halves – 'Flower Garden' and 'Kitchen Garden' – each with perimeter walks. Structures are indicated at the western end of the northern Terrace Walk, at the north-west corners of the flower and kitchen gardens, and at the south-east corner of the kitchen garden. It also records the main stable block to the west of the house.

The 1884 sale particulars refer to detached stabling, yard, outbuildings, vinery and greenhouse, walled kitchen garden, lawn tennis ground and flower garden. By 1920 the garden had 'extensive flower borders and walled fruit trees', 'charming old-world terraces', 'prolific walled kitchen garden with a quantity of matured fruit trees in full bearing', two vineries, a peach-house and three long ranges of heated shelters for tender plants. Photographs contemporary with these two sales confirm abundant, mature planting, and show the tennis lawn in active use, and the glasshouses.

THE GARDEN TODAY

The southern part of the garden is the least altered. A path runs from the wrought-iron gates to what was the principal entrance to the house until about 1800. In summer the overhead false acacias (*Robinia pseudoacacia*) cast dappled shade on the gravel path and lawn. The heavy backdrop of ivy, holly, arbutus, bay, aucuba, holm oak, *Viburnum tinus* and acanthus screen the boundary walls and provide contrast to the light foliage of the robinias above. The nineteenth-century flower-beds have gone, but hedges of common box were planted in the 1980s not only to frame the entrance, but also to lead one to either side.

To the north of the house, the garden you see today reflects changes made by the National Trust over a period of more than ten years from 1982. The aim was to give back to the garden, whose planting had gone beyond maturity, a relaxed 'Old English' style within the seventeenth-century structure, as well as to provide successive colour and interest throughout the year within the main flower garden. So you now enter through a yew arbour, which lends an element of surprise to what is on the other side.

The eastern terrace walk is lined with agapanthus in tubs, linked in summer by a haze of catmint. A thick box hedge surrounds a border with a

The kitchen garden

(Above) View of the house from the northern terrace

soft pink, blue, silver and soft yellow colour scheme, containing fuchsias, phlox, agapanthus, eryngiums, hemerocallis and rudbeckias, backed by the road wall. An old espalier pear tree 'Louise Bonne of Jersey' grows on the wall with *Rosa* 'Lady Hillingdon', *Clematis* 'Alba Luxurians' and 'Madame Julia Correvon' and *Ribes speciosum*.

The northern terrace walk has an autumn border which principally contains asters and vines, and leads to a wisteria border. The greatest surprise from here is the sight of the sunken garden below the terrace, and especially the lower kitchen garden.

Steps at either end of the terrace lead respectively to the main lawn and sunken garden. The former can be reached via a short avenue of standard hollies, leading to the main lawn, which is bordered by holly cones (*Ilex aquifolium* 'Argentea Marginata') and, on the left of the path, a border of dwarf shrubs – Cistus and summer and spring bulbs (crinums, nerines and lilies). Beyond the tall yew hedge lies the rose garden, approached by a semicircular flight of steps. The roses are in shades of yellow, soft white and pink. The double borders of July flowers above the rose garden steps lead to a narrow, enclosed yew passage and down to the garden's most charming feature – a sunken, walled oasis of orchard, glasshouse, culinary herb border, cut-flower beds and vegetables.

In spring the lawn below the orchard is transformed into a flowery meadow of *Scilla siberica*, *Anemone blanda*, *Muscari*, *Chionodoxa forbesii*, dwarf *Narcissus* 'Hawera' and jonquils. The vegetable and cut-flower area is surrounded by espalier apples, including old varieties 'Pitmaston Pine Apple', 'Beauty of Bath', 'Devonshire Quarrenden', underplanted in spring with forget-me-nots and tulips. Beyond is the southern boundary to the yard, screened almost entirely by an old fig, which overhangs the lead cistern. The west boundary wall is planted with white-flowering plants and climbers such as *Clematis* 'Huldine', and variegated foliage plants.

23

FENTON HOUSE AND ITS OWNERS

THE SEVENTEENTH CENTURY

Fenton House stands on manorial land. Between 1682 and 1690 there were four lords of the manor, with the last one being a minor of six. This must help explain why the manorial records, which should hold information on the building of the house, are patchy and confusing. However, they suggest that it was built around 1686 by William Eades 'in a place called Mill Hill and adjoining a place called Ostend', and that it passed to Thomas Simpson in 1689. A brick in one of the chimneystacks is dated 1693. William Eades's father was a bricklayer, which may explain why the house looks as though it was designed by a master carpenter or bricklayer rather than an architect.

THE EIGHTEENTH CENTURY

In 1706 Joshua Gee bought Fenton House. He had in that same year married a rich widow, Anna Osgood, and their alliance is commemorated with their initials on the south gates. Both had children from first marriages, and produced another four, so that at one point the house held nine children. Gee was a Quaker linen merchant and also traded in iron ore. He was one of the founding partners of the Principio Company, which had been formed to produce pig-iron in Maryland for sale in England. At a later stage he went into partnership with George Washington's father in this enterprise. He had several connections with America as one of the original mortgagees of Pennsylvania, being part of a consortium of six British businessmen who raised £6,000 to get William Penn out of debt, using the State of Pennsylvania as security. He is still remembered in America for his book *The Trade and Navigation of Great-Britain Considered* (1729), which went into seven editions in the eighteenth century. He was an adviser to the Board of Trade and Plantations, and his book's subtitle states his position: 'That the surest way for a Nation to increase in Riches, is to prevent the Importation of such Foreign Commodities as may be raised at Home' and 'That this Kingdom is capable of raising within itself, and its Colonies, Materials for employing all our Poor in those Manufactures, which we now import from such of our Neighbours who refuse the Admission of ours.'

Joshua Gee's oldest son, also called Joshua, became an ironmaster in Shropshire, with a forge at Attingham which made kettles and buckets. The younger Joshua received substantial sums from both his father and his grandfather, which he seems to have squandered. Certainly, Gee senior rewrote his Will to reduce his eldest son's inheritance, and on his death in 1730 left Fenton House to his nineteen-year-old younger son, Osgood.

After Osgood Gee had married in 1737, he went to live in Bromley, and certainly from 1750 to 1755

he let the house. So the Notice of Sale he issued in 1756 probably reflects how the place was in his father's day:

… a substantial brick building, containing four very good Rooms on a Floor, two Stair-Cases, with exceeding good lower Offices, which are remarkably dry, and two Wine Vaults; the Out-Offices are of Brick, apart from the House, and consist of two Coach-Houses, two four-stall stables, with Servants Rooms over them, a Brewhouse, a pleasant garden well planted with Fruit-Trees, and a Kitchen-Garden, all inclos'd with a substantial Brick Wall.

It was during the tenure of the next owner, Mary Martin, that the house was named Clock House, presumably because a clock was added to the east front where the disk is today. She was also responsible for building a greenhouse in the garden.

Mary Martin (?1705–65) came from a naval family. Married in 1726 to Captain (later Admiral) William Martin, she came to live at Fenton House only as a widow. After two other owners, John Hyndman and John Bond, the house was bought by Philip Fenton in 1793, and it remained in this family's ownership until 1834.

Mary Martin; *painted by Allan Ramsay in 1761, when she was living at Fenton House (Birmingham Museum & Art Gallery)*

(Left)
Fenton House and garden appear as plot 292 on the 1762 manorial map of Hampstead. They have changed little since

James and Margaret Fenton and their children; *painted in Riga by Friedrich Hartmann Barisien (private collection). His uncle Philip, who bought the house that now bears their name in 1793, appears in the oval portrait on the wall*

THE NINETEENTH CENTURY

Philip Fenton (1734–1806) was a Yorkshireman whose father had dealt in coal. He went out to Riga (then in Russia) and became a Baltic merchant, exporting to England. He was joined by his nephew James (1754–1834), who was married in Riga in 1779 and whose seven children were all born there. In 1793 Philip Fenton returned to England and bought the Clock House. James and all his family joined him four years later. During their occupation, the house gained a reputation for hospitality. A friend recalled James and his wife Margaret as being 'quite specimens of old Patriarchal days, with the modern adjuncts of butler, footmen and "state" of the present day'. One of their four daughters, also Margaret, kept a diary for the year 1796. She and her younger sisters attended day school in Hampstead, while having separate masters for music and drawing. Weekly dancing classes were held at their house, to which neighbours were welcomed, and came as a social occasion. Friends and relatives came to dinner, and the children went to balls.

It was perhaps after Philip Fenton's death in 1806, and James's inheritance, that alterations were made to the house that seem to date from the period. The most notable is the addition of the colonnaded porch between the two projecting wings on the east front. An arch and columns were also added along the northern end of the Blue Porcelain Room, probably instead of a passage wall, to make it larger. And of course the Fentons also gave their name to the house. It is not known when this happened, but it was certainly by 1860.

In 1829 James Fenton presided over a meeting of Hampstead tenants at the nearby Hollybush Inn to protest against building on the Heath. In that year Sir Thomas Maryon Wilson, Lord of the Manor, tried to obtain a private Act of Parliament to break the restrictions preventing him from engaging in building development. The public battle was won only when his heir, Sir John, ceded his manorial rights for £45,000 in 1871, and the Heath passed into public ownership.

The Heath's cause was taken up by another owner of Fenton House. Thomas Turner (1805–83) led a deputation on behalf of the Metropolitan Board of Works concerned with securing the Heath as a place of recreation. After he left Fenton House in 1858, there followed a period when the place was let out to a rapid succession of people, which ended only when George Trewby (1839–1910) bought it in 1884.

The 1884 sale particulars for Fenton House describe it as a 'commodious detached residence ... pleasantly situate in this favourite and healthy Residential Locality'. Close to the Heath, Christ Church, several railway stations and an easy drive to both the City and the West End, it was, unsurprisingly, described as 'desirable'. The rooms are listed in the same configuration as today, but still with their closets. The basement contained the Kitchen, Scullery, Housekeeper's Room and Butler's Pantry. The garden included a tennis lawn and 'ornamental flower garden with terrace'. Interestingly, the particulars also include the 'covered approach from the gate to the front door'. This was a curved, ribbed metal affair, which Lady Binning removed.

George Trewby had made his career in the gas industry, becoming in 1858 gas engineer to the Ottoman Empire in Constantinople. He returned to England in 1862 and worked for the Gas Light & Coke Company, most notably in 1870–8 at the new Beckton Gas Works. By 1884, when he bought Fenton House, he was Construction and Carbonising Engineer for the company.

May Trewby's wedding at Fenton House in 1902. George Trewby is the white-bearded figure on the right-hand side of the front row

THE TWENTIETH CENTURY

Mrs Trewby sold the house in 1920 to a stock-broker, Eustace Young, who in turn let it to Robert Brousson in 1922. He turned the Porcelain Room into a kitchen and created a billiard-room down-stairs, but neither arrangement lasted beyond his tenure.

Katherine, Lady Binning (1871–1952) bought Fenton House in 1936, but allowed the Broussons to continue living there until 1937, when she let it to a Dr Abercrombie. Her husband, heir to the Earl of Haddington, had died in 1917 and she spent a good deal of time at his family's country houses in the Scottish Borders, Tyninghame and Mellerstain. She particularly loved the former, and all her staff in London were Scottish, but the London climate was clearly more favourable. She seems to have retained her mother's house at 49 Berkeley Square until about 1934, and was already living in Hampstead when she bought Fenton House.

After her husband's death, Lady Binning seems to have led a relatively lonely life, surrounded princi-pally by the collection she had inherited from her mother (see p. 30). The Trust's first Historic Buildings Secretary, James Lees-Milne, described her as 'elderly, delicate and hot-housey', while the plumber's son, Terry Bowley, remembers her as rather eccentric and dressed in Victorian clothes. He found it a sad house and felt Lady Binning was really happiest in Scotland. James Lees-Milne visited her several times and they seem to have come to like each other.

Lady Binning's solicitor was first in touch with the National Trust in December 1938. The Second World War intervened, and it was not until 1944 that she herself wrote to James Lees-Milne. Her idea was that Fenton House should become a museum to display her porcelain collection, which she had previously intended to bequeath to the Victoria & Albert Museum. On her death in 1952 Lady Binning left Fenton House to the National Trust, which decided to rehouse the Benton Fletcher Collection of keyboard instruments at Fenton, as their home had been destroyed in the war.

Early photographs of the Benton Fletcher instru-ments at Fenton House show them sitting awk-

The Blue Porcelain Room in 1950, when it was Lady Binning's Bedroom

The Drawing Room, as redecorated by John Fowler in 1973

wardly amongst Lady Binning's possessions. Those of her things which had come from the Haddington houses returned there on her death, which left some rooms looking rather bare. In 1973 the Trust took the decision to rethink the arrangement of the rooms and their decoration, and enlisted John Fowler's help. The aim was to bring out the qualities of the place and give it more the feeling of a lived-in home. The choice of colours and materials, and the way they were applied, sought to give a mellow feel about the place and to avoid making it look newly decorated. Since then, some contents have occasionally been added to fill remaining gaps. The garden was similarly revived by the National Trust from 1982.

Katherine,
Lady Binning

29

THE COLLECTORS

Today's visitor to Fenton House can be left in little doubt that the contents were accumulated by years of dedicated collecting. Eighteenth-century Oriental and European porcelain, satinwood furniture and needlework dominate this collection of decorative art, which represents a popular, but conservative, neo-Georgian taste that was prevalent in the early twentieth century. The diversity of the collection left to the National Trust with the house in 1952 results from the passions and circumstances of three collectors: George Salting (1835–1909), his sister-in-law, Mrs Millicent E. Salting (d.1924) and her daughter Katherine, Lady Binning (1871–1952).

Additionally, the Benton Fletcher collection of early keyboard instruments and the Peter Barkworth collection of English pictures and paintings has broadened the range and deepened the value of Fenton House as the home of domestic collections of great charm and historical interest.

GEORGE SALTING

Lady Binning's uncle, George Salting, was one of the great art collectors of the nineteenth century. Despite his vast wealth, derived from sheep stations in Australia, he lived modestly and was generous in loaning out his collection. On his death, he bequeathed superb early Oriental ceramics and Renaissance bronzes to the Victoria & Albert Museum, rare prints and drawings to the British Museum, and Old Master paintings to the National Gallery. Although the residue of his estate went to his niece, Lady Binning, exactly which items at Fenton House came from Salting remains uncertain. He most probably contributed the striking collection of Chinese blue-and-white porcelain displayed in the Blue Porcelain Room, much of which appears in the 1914 inventory.

MILLICENT SALTING

If the Fenton House collection was inspired and founded by George Salting, then the growth and Georgian character of the collection may be attributed to Millicent Salting. The majority of the contents have been identified in the 1914 inventory of her home at 49 Berkeley Square, which was written by George Stoner, of the porcelain dealers Stoner & Evans. The catalogue describes over 1,600 items. Many types of objects, such as the English pottery and porcelain 'toys', are unlike anything known to have been collected by George Salting, and more akin to the tastes of contemporary women collectors like Lady Charlotte Schreiber.

Millicent Salting (née Browne) was the wife of George's brother William, who inherited part of the Salting family's lucrative business. While it has long been assumed that her collection came directly from George Salting, it is now clear that she collected in her own right. A number of important pieces were purchased at auction in the years after George Salting's death in 1909. These include the figures of the Rustic Seasons and part of the tea

George Salting, part of whose vast collection is now at Fenton House

and coffee service made in 1774 for Jane Burke, the wife of the politician Edmund Burke – all Bristol porcelain sold from the Trapnell Collection in 1913. Like her brother-in-law, Mrs Salting was generous in loaning and bequeathing items to public collections.

LADY BINNING

Thus, it fell to Lady Binning to be the 'editor' of the collection. From annotations to the 1914 inventory, we know that much of Mrs Salting's furniture was sold, though the pretty painted satin-wood secretaire and the tables in the Drawing Room were among those pieces that were retained. A substantial selection of pottery and porcelain was lent to the Royal Museum of Scotland in 1928. These items, which included the Bristol Burke Service (the Rustic Seasons remain at Fenton), were given to the museum on Lady Binning's death in 1952.

In spite of dividing the collection, Lady Binning continued to make some acquisitions. In December 1938 she purchased Meissen figures of a harlequin and a miner from the dealers Hyman of Brompton Road. Lady Binning also probably bought Meissen service wares, plus a few figures and animals, as these items do not appear in the 1914 inventory. More than her individual purchases, it was Lady Binning's thoughtful management of her inheritances which has left these great legacies of decorative art in London and Edinburgh.

GEORGE BENTON FLETCHER

Given his background, Benton Fletcher (1866–1944) seemed an unlikely early music enthusiast. His diverse careers had included soldier, social worker and archaeologist. When, influenced by his acquaintance with two founders of the National Trust, he fixed upon collecting early keyboard instruments, he was motivated by a wider concern for the preservation of all significant works of art, and by a deep-rooted patriotism. Finding significant examples of early keyboard instruments, having them restored, played and heard, then became the consuming passion of his life. Well before the early music revival had gained widespread popularity in England, Benton Fletcher advocated performing music on the instruments for which it had been conceived.

In 1934 he bought Old Devonshire House in Bloomsbury, creating an early music centre where students and professional musicians could meet, practise and perform. After giving the house and collection to the National Trust in 1937, Major Fletcher remained in residence, continuing to foster musical activities. At the outbreak of war, most of the collection was moved to the Cotswolds; it proved a timely transfer, as Old Devonshire House perished in an air raid.

In 1943 Major Fletcher and the National Trust purchased 3 Cheyne Walk as a new centre, but Benton Fletcher died before these plans were realised. When the National Trust acquired Fenton House in 1952, the instruments were moved to these more spacious surroundings. As Benton Fletcher would have wished, accredited students still come to practise, and there are regular concerts.

The richly decorated Italian harpsichord in the South-East Room is part of the Benton Fletcher collection of keyboard instruments

PETER BARKWORTH

Peter Barkworth (1929–2006), actor, was a familiar figure in Hampstead, where he lived for over 40 years. He was also familiar to countless theatregoers and television viewers; to the former he was probably best known for his leading role as King Edward VIII in *Crown Matrimonial* at the Haymarket Theatre in the early 1970s, and to the latter as Kenneth Bligh in *The Power Game* or as the high-flying banker in *Telford's Change*.

The stage may have been his first love but collecting art was a lifelong passion, and at his death he bequeathed 55 works to Fenton House, only ten minutes' walk from his home in Flask.

Barkworth's selection was personal and instinctive, rather than scholarly, and reflects his own interests and loves – the theatre, Hampstead (and by extension Camden Town) and the English countryside and coast, the last perhaps a legacy of his early childhood in Margate.

The core, and most dominant part, is a collection of oil paintings by members of the Camden Town Group, including a classic Harold Gilman *Still Life with Pears and a Plate*, a 1910 Spencer Gore painting of *A Frenchwoman* seated confrontationally facing the viewer, and *La ci Darem la Mano*, a Mozartian subject taken from Don Giovanni by Walter Sickert, one of four pieces by this artist.

The marine and topographical works are mostly in pencil or watercolour. Barkworth's taste in drawings and watercolours seems to have veered between the precise and the spontaneous. Among the former is a group of works attributed to Samuel Prout and a beautiful soft chalk drawing, *Trees at Thorpe near Norwich* by John Sell Cotman. Outstanding among the freer works are a remarkable study by Edward Duncan, *Sunset over the Mumbles*, executed with perhaps a dozen strokes of a heavily laden brush, and a delightful coastal scene, *The Moor by the Sea* by William McTaggart.

A little Constable oil, *Cumulus Clouds over a Landscape*, links these twin interests and despite, or maybe because of, the fact that it contains no identifiable topographical features, Barkworth liked to think that it was painted in Hampstead, within a short stroll of Constable's own house in Well Walk.

Two pictures by Charles Ginner feature Hampstead: *Pond Street* is a heavy pen drawing filled in with watercolour, in a manner somewhat reminiscent of cloisonné enamelling; and a gloriously murky night scene of Flask Walk seen from the elevated vantage point of Ginner's studio above a shop on Hampstead High Street. These among all the others will help to ensure the enduring legacy of a collector who loved Hampstead.

English actor Peter Barkworth (1929–2006) with the Best Actor BAFTA he won in 1978 for his roles in *Professional Foul* and *The Country Party*. (Photo by John Downing (Getty Images)